THE LITTLE COFFEE BOOK

Jennie Reekie

PIATKUS

Other titles in the series

The Little Green Avocado Book
The Little Garlic Book
The Little Pepper Book
The Little Lemon Book
The Little Apple Book
The Little Strawberry Book
The Little Mushroom Book
The Little Nut Book
The Little Bean Book
The Little Honey Book
The Little Mustard Book
The Little Rice Book
The Little Tea Book

© 1985 Judy Piatkus (Publishers) Limited

Reprinted 1990

British Library Cataloguing in Publication Data

Reekie, Jennie
    The little coffee book.
    1. Coffee
    I. Title
    641.3'373   TX415
    ISBN 0-86188-344-6

Drawings by Linda Broad
Designed by Ken Leeder
Cover illustrated by Lynne Robinson

Typeset by Phoenix Photosetting, Chatham
Printed and bound by The Bath Press, Avon

CONTENTS

'Black as the devil,
Hot as hell,
Pure as an angel
Sweet as love.'

Talleyrand (1754–1838)

THE HISTORY OF COFFEE

T here are several stories – some might say fairy
stories – about the origin of coffee, of which the
most popular and best known is that of Kaldi, the
Yemeni goatherd. One night when Kaldi was
tending his goats he noticed that instead of being
their usual placid selves, they were dancing excit-
edly near a bush which bore a number of bright red
berries. Kaldi decided to taste the berries, and it
wasn't long before he was dancing too!

News of Kaldi and his goats quickly spread to the
local monastery, where the Immam was having a
problem keeping himself and his dervishes awake
during the night's prayer vigil. The Immam thought

1

he would try these exotic berries to see if they would help – with great success! They all managed to stay wide awake for their prayers, with their faculties intact, if not heightened. News of this remarkable discovery went from monastery to monastery from the Yemen throughout the Arab world to Cairo, Medina and to Mecca.

Commemorating this event in a poem written in 1718, Abbé Massieu wrote:

The monks each in turn, as the evening draws near,
Drink round the great cauldron – a circle of cheer!
And the dawn in amaze, revisiting that shore,
On idle beds of ease surprised them nevermore!

Another story concerns Ali bin Omar al Shadhilly, who must have had something to do with the introduction of coffee as to this day he is the patron saint of Arab coffee growers and drinkers, and in Algeria coffee is known as *shadhiliye* after him. It is said that, having been charged with misconduct with the king's daughter, he was banished into the mountains with some of his servants. There, for want of anything else to drink, they boiled up some coffee berries in water. Many of the inhabitants of the nearby villages were suffering from an epidemic of itching, and Shadhilly was able to cure them with his concoction. As a result he was pardoned and allowed to return home, where presumably he continued to brew coffee. In fact, some of the first mentions of coffee in the Arab world refer to it as a medicine.

Coffee was being cultivated in the Yemen in the sixth century, but it was not until the thirteenth century that the beans were roasted and made into anything resembling the drink we know today. The first coffee house was opened in Mecca in the late fifteenth century, and coffee became so popular that it took the place of the forbidden alcohol. Mohammed had given it his blessing by saying that after his first cup he felt able 'to unseat forty horsemen and possess fifty women.'

Fairly understandably, the Arabs were reluctant to relinquish their monopoly of the coffee market. They forbade any bean to be exported from Arabia unless it had first been boiled or parched, so that it was infertile. However, where there's a will . . . and an Indian, Baba Budan, bound seven seeds to his body, smuggled them out and planted them on his land at Chikamalgur in Southern India. It was from the progeny of these trees that the Dutch took seeds to start their plantations in Java, which for many years were among the most important in the world.

The first coffee came to Europe – to Italy – at the beginning of the seventeenth century. At first it was received with mixed feelings as many people felt that Satan, having forbidden the Moslems (who were thought to be his followers) to drink wine because it was used in Holy Communion, had given them coffee instead. Some of the priests who had become coffee enthusiasts appealed to the Pope to give his verdict. The Pope, on tasting it, declared: 'Why,

3

this Satan's drink is so delicious that it would be a pity to let the infidels have exclusive use of it. We shall cheat Satan by baptising it.' Which he duly did, and so made it 'safe' for Christians to drink.

From Italy coffee spread to France and Holland and on to England, and by the latter part of the seventeenth century coffee houses and cafés had been established in all the major European cities.

COFFEE HOUSES

As coffee drinking heightens and stimulates the senses, coffee houses have always been a meeting place for intellectuals, poets, writers and artists. The Turks called their coffee houses 'schools of the wise', whilst in seventeenth-century England they became known as 'penny universities', because that was how much it cost to get in. It is said that the seeds of the French revolution were sown in the Café

Foy in Paris, and those of the American in the Green Dragon in Boston!

The first coffee house in Europe was opened in Oxford in 1650 by a Turkish Jew, followed two years later by one in St Michael's Alley, Cornhill. This was the start of the great coffee house boom which was to sweep through England for a century and was to result in the founding of such illustrious institutions as The Stock Exchange, The Baltic Exchange and Lloyds Insurance, all of which had their beginnings in coffee houses where men of similar interests gathered.

Having made such a strong initial impact in Britain, we are the one country in Europe where the tradition of the coffee bar and café has not survived to any real extent, despite a brief revival in the 1950s. There are three reasons for this. First, the coffee houses, which had begun in Cromwell's time, started to change in character, selling alcohol as well as coffee, and became less appealing venues. Secondly, and more importantly, at this time none of the British colonies grew coffee and it was therefore an expensive import via the Dutch and French. Also the founding of the East India Company meant that the Government was keen to foster the tea trade and it did everything in its power to encourage tea drinking and discourage coffee drinking. Thirdly, it is easier to brew a good pot of tea than a good pot of coffee!

COFFEE HEROES

The way in which coffee reached the Caribbean and, from there, South America is a story of fortitude and heroism. In 1715 Louis XIV, who was a passionate coffee lover, asked the Dutch, who owed him a favour, to procure him a coffee tree from Java for the botanical garden in Paris. A special greenhouse was constructed for it and the plant duly blossomed and bore fruit.

A Frenchman, Chevalier Gabriel Mathiew de Clieu, was determined to take a seedling across the Atlantic to the French colony of Martinique so that he could found coffee plantations there. However, his request for a seedling was refused, but by subterfuge he managed to obtain one and set out on his journey. It was by any standards an appalling

voyage: one of the passengers teased de Clieu unmercifully about his little plant and tore off one of its fragile branches. But undeterred, through storms, attacks by pirates, and finally becalmed, de Clieu continued to nurse his precious plant. He even shared his water ration with it. He arrived in Martinique in 1720, planted his seedling and 50 years later there were 18,791,680 trees flourishing there.

Perhaps the most romantic coffee story of all relates to coffee and Brazil. On hearing of the success of coffee trees in the French colonies, the Brazilian Emperor wanted to plant them in his country, but the French, in much the same way as the Arabs had done earlier, wished to protect their interests and would not export plants or seeds. The Emperor rather wisely sent a good-looking emissary, Francisco de Melho Palheta, to French Guinea to see if he could persuade them to let him have some plants. Palheta's quest would have failed had his charm not matched his looks. He quickly enchanted the Governor's wife, who, before he sailed home for Brazil, sent him a bunch of flowers in which was embedded a small coffee plant – and so was founded the world's greatest coffee empire!

FACTS AND FIGURES

C offee is of immense importance in both world
trade and economics and is second only to oil in
the world commodity market. Over 100 million
cups of coffee are drunk throughout the world in a
day, and the coffee industry employs over 20 million
people.

The total world production of coffee for 1982/3
was 96,875,000 60-kilo sacks of green beans, of
which 74,484,000 were Arabicas, and 22,391,000
were Robustas. Brazil is still by far the biggest pro-
ducer with 29,400,000 sacks, followed by Colombia
with 13,500,000. 2,522,000 bags of green beans,
worth 3,527,836 US dollars, were imported into
Britain.

By far the highest per capita consumption is in
Scandinavia – with Finland heading the list for 1982
with 12.77 kilos per person per annum, followed by
Sweden on 11.73, Denmark on 11.46 and Norway
on 10.51, which is 2.49 kilos ahead of Austria on
7.92. The consumption in France is 5.94, the
United States 4.77 and Italy 4.36.

Britain's consumption is one of the lowest on
2.46, but this is an increase on the 1975 figure of
2.16. It works out at 2.23 cups per day per person
over the age of 15. When the fact that 30 per cent of
the population rarely drink coffee is taken into
account, that figure rises to 3.15 cups per day. The
highest consumption is in the 30 to 39 year-old age
bracket.

GROWING COFFEE

C offee is cultivated in over 50 countries, but as it is killed by frost it can only be grown between the tropics of Cancer and Capricorn. It dislikes intense heat and strong sunlight, so taller trees are frequently grown in the plantations to provide shade. There are two main varieties of coffee plant – the *Coffea arabica*, which originated in Ethiopia and still grows wild there and in parts of the Yemen, and *Coffea canephora* or *Coffea robusta*.

The best beans are those produced by the Arabica tree, which grows at between 3,300 and 6,000 feet, and the best of these are the ones grown at the higher altitudes.

The Robusta (as it name implies) is a sturdier plant, indigenous to the Congo where it was found growing in 1898. It is less susceptible to disease and will survive with only small amounts of rainfall. Beans from the Robusta are cheaper to produce, so they are often added to the more expensive Arabica beans to keep the price down, and they are used to produce instant coffee.

The tree or shrub is similar to a camellia. In the wild, the Arabica will grown to 20 feet but they are generally kept to about six feet to make them easier to harvest and to conserve their energy for producing beans. In countries where there is a wet season followed by a dry one, the trees tend to flower all at once; in those with an even rainfall they flower throughout the year. The blossom, which has a strong smell of jasmine, lasts for only about three days before it falls and the berries are formed. Coffee trees are rather unusual in that at any one time they may bear flowers, green, un-ripe berries and ripe, dark red berries, or cherries as they are called – a process which takes six months.

The trees start bearing fruit when they are between three and five years old. Although they can continue to flourish until they are over 100, they produce their best crops during the first 15 years. It is difficult to be precise about the yield of a tree as so much depends on the soil and climate, quite apart from how well it is generally cared for and pruned, but just over two pounds is average.

HARVESTING AND CLEANING

Harvesting is a long and laborious process as all the berries do not ripen at the same time, and will not ripen once they have been picked. A skilled picker can only harvest 176 lb in a day, which will produce 30 lb of dry coffee beans. Despite being so labour intensive, hand picking is always done for the high-grade coffees as it ensures that only the ripe berries are picked.

In some of the larger plantations, for the cheaper coffees, they strip-pick the trees. This not only produces an inferior coffee as inevitably some of the under-ripe and over-ripe beans find their way into the dried beans, but it severely damages the trees from which they take two years to recover.

In parts of Africa the ripe berries are harvested by placing a very large cloth under the tree and then shaking the tree vigorously so that the ripe berries fall into the cloth. The berries are then sieved to remove dust, twigs, leaves, stones, etc.

The berry, or cherry which is what it closely resembles, is a round fruit. Inside a rather gummy pulp lie the two coffee seeds, which are pressed together like a round bean. This is covered by a husk, known as parchment, under which lies a semi-transparent 'silver skin'.

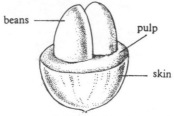

There are two methods of cleaning the beans – the dry and the wet methods. In the dry, or natural, method the beans are spread in thin layers and left to dry in the sun and are raked and turned regularly so that they dry evenly. It is then easy to remove both the shrivelled husk and the parchment, either by machine or, in the more primitive areas, with a grind-stone.

When the beans are prepared by the wet, or washed, method, a machine first removes the gummy pulp, then the beans are soaked in natural enzymes which cause the husks to ferment, after which it is easy to wash them off. The beans are then dried, either in the sun, or in a mechanical drier, so that just the thin silver skin remains. Sometimes in very high grade coffees this is left on to provide the beans with some protection during travelling, but it is generally removed by a huller. Finally the beans are picked over, graded and lightly polished to give them an attractive appearance, and packed into sacks ready for export.

Washed coffees are generally considered superior to natural coffees, as it is easier for the latter to become musty or have other faults if they are not carefully and evenly dried. But some coffee connoisseurs consider the best natural coffees to have a better flavour, and the beans certainly age better.

COFFEE GRADING AND BLENDING

C offee beans are graded according to the size of the bean, how it was harvested and cleaned and where it was grown. This not only relates to the country and the region, but also to the altitude, as this affects the hardness of the bean. Apart from one or two exceptions, such as Sumatran Mandheling, hard bean coffees command a higher price than soft.

There are two reasons for blending coffee – economics and flavour. By adding some cheaper Robustas or Brazilian Arabicas, for example, to high quality Arabica beans, it is possible to keep the price of a coffee down, without it being detrimental to the end product. Equally, by blending together a number of different beans (sometimes it is just two or three, but more often it is eight or more), it is possible to produce a coffee which has a complete and rounded flavour, bringing out the best qualities in each of the beans. Coffee blending is an extremely skilful job which requires a highly sensitive palate to produce the best blends.

BUYING YOUR BEANS

B uying the beans is undoubtedly the most important part of producing a good cup of coffee. If you start off with inferior beans (i.e. poor quality, badly and unevenly roasted, stale, etc), you will never be able to brew coffee successfully. The easiest way to buy is to play safe and choose a branded blend, many of which are excellent and from which you should always achieve a uniform result. But experimenting with different coffees is both fun and interesting. The problem is that once you step into the realms of speciality coffees, you are confronted with so many different names, blends and descriptions (like buying wine) that it is often difficult to know where to start and to a certain extent coffee buying has to be a matter of trial and error.

The first thing to remember is that coffee must be fresh. Buy it from a shop which roasts its own (see page 18), or if they buy ready-roasted, has a rapid turnover. If coffee has been vacuum packed it will

14

obviously keep longer, but otherwise roasted beans should be used within a month of roasting. If you buy beans and ask for them to be ground, do not keep it for more than a week.

It is impossible to give any sort of description of blended coffees as they are dependent on the whim of the blender and will vary considerably from supplier to supplier. However, the following descriptions from the London Coffee Information Centre are a good guide to some of the most common pure coffees.

Brazilian Santos: A high quality coffee grown in the Sao Paulo region, which has a special individual flavour. It is a smooth, full-bodied coffee with little bitterness or acidity.

Colombian Medellin Excelso: This fine coffee is high grown in the Medellin area of Colombia. It is full-bodied and has less acidity than most Colombian coffee. It is a delicious mellow coffee, slightly nutty in flavour.

Costa Rican Tapuzza: A delightfully mild coffee with a delicate acidity. Especially good for breakfast.

Ethiopian Mocha: The home of the original coffee plant still produces superb coffee such as this. It has a distinctly different flavour which is often described as 'gamey'. Traditionally, it is used for Turkish coffee.

Jamaican Blue Mountain: One of the world's most celebrated and expensive coffees. Relatively difficult to buy the real thing, beware of copies. It has a perfect, subtle balance, full-bodied, rich in flavour with a wonderful aroma and mild acidity. There are many blends available, which may or may not contain the real thing.

Java: Coffee from Java is relatively difficult to find. It is usually well-matured before roasting, giving it a unique flavour which is slightly 'smoky'. A very distinguished coffee, often the choice of gourmets.

Kenya: A very fine African coffee and probably the most widely known in the UK. It is famous for its beautiful aroma, its strong flavour and sharp acidity. A good all-purpose coffee.

Mysore: Grown in the south of India, it is full-bodied and has a rich flavour, often described as 'winey'. Mysore coffee is often blended with Mocha coffee and known as Mysore Mocha.

Nicaragua: This delicious coffee from Central America is very popular on the Continent and often used in blends. It is excellent 'pure' – discover its mild non-acidic characteristics, ideal for a breakfast coffee.

Tanzanian Kilimanjaro: Tanzanian coffee tends to be stronger than Central American coffee, but without the sharpness of Kenyan coffee. Coffee grown in the Kilimanjaro area is often known as Chagga coffee; the mountain air and the volcanic soil of the area gives the coffee a distinctive, well-balanced flavour.

Sumatra: Coffee from the Dutch East Indies, famous for its distinctive flavour. It is often dark-roasted and has a heavy mellow flavour with little acidity. It is similar to *Java* coffee.

ROASTING AND GRINDING

T he unroasted coffee bean is almost completely flavourless. In the roasting process the volatile coffee oil is released, spreading itself throughout the bean as it pushes its way to the surface and releases its flavour. The longer the bean is roasted, the further the oil is pushed out – thus, dark roasted beans have a shinier surface than lighter roasts.

As with any other bean or nut, the coffee bean is a combination of fibre, fat, protein, minerals, vitamins and, of course, caffeine. Good roasting is important if the flavour of all these substances is to be subtly brought out and not destroyed. For example, the heavy French roasts are not only less acid than some lighter roasts, they also contain less caffeine as some of this becomes burnt off during increased roasting. This explains why Continentals happily drink dark black coffee in the evening without it appearing to stop them from sleeping!

The type of roast you choose is entirely a matter of individual preference, although most people prefer a lighter roast for morning than for after dinner. Unlike wine, in which acidity is a fault, in coffee it is considered an attribute. Acidity is largely dependent on where the bean was grown, but it is also related to the degree of roasting and the lighter roasts are more acid than the dark Continental ones.

Light roasts require the best quality Arabica beans, so that their full delicate flavour can be easily distinguished. In a medium roast, stronger beans are used producing a stronger coffee, whilst in a full roast any acidity will have left the beans and there is a slightly more bitter flavour. When it comes to the high, Continental or double roast, slightly poorer quality beans are used, as the delicacy is lost and replaced by a strong, noticeably charcoal, flavour.

Most commercial roasters consist of a large rotating drum which is heated by gas jets to 260°C/500°F. Inside the coffee beans are tossed around so that they roast evenly to the desired colour. Roasting is a skilled job, requiring both knowledge and intuition to make sure the beans are roasted to perfection.

Having said it is a skilled job, it is perfectly possible to roast beans yourself at home provided that you don't mind your kitchen (and the rest of your house as well) smelling very strongly of roast coffee for a couple of days! There are a few home roasters on the market, but beans can be roasted either in a frying pan or in the oven. The advantages of roasting one's own beans are firstly the price, as green beans are considerably cheaper than ready-roasted ones, and secondly, green beans keep for a long time.

The first thing you must decide is where you are going to put the beans when they are ready as it is important to *halt the cooking process immediately*. A marble surface is ideal, otherwise tip them on to a heat resistant surface or newspaper and cool them quickly with cold air from a hair drier. Any loose husk, etc should be removed, and once the beans are cold they can be ground. The whole beans should be stored as soon as possible in an airtight container.

Before you start roasting, take a couple of beans of your favourite roast and keep them nearby so that you can compare their colour as the beans start to darken.

Don't worry if you don't achieve a very even roast, but discard any that appear to be burnt as they would impart an unpleasant flavour to the coffee.

ON TOP OF THE COOKER

Using a large, heavy frying pan, place it on top of the cooker over a moderate to fairly high heat. (The exact heat will depend on the thickness of the pan.) Add the beans in a single layer for more even browning. Keep shaking the pan and turning the beans, using a wooden spoon, until they are the desired colour. If you want a dark roast, increase the heat to maximum so that they brown quickly.

IN THE OVEN

This is likely to give you a more even roast and slightly less smell! Heat the oven to 260°C/500°F. Place a tin in the pre-heated oven for two to three minutes. Add the beans, scattering them in a single layer, and 'roast' them for 10 minutes. Remove from the oven, stir and replace, then continue cooking, removing the beans every two minutes to give them a good stir until they are the required colour.

In some parts of the world the unroasted green, coffee bean is fermented into wine. Also newly picked beans are pounded with fats or bananas and turned into food.

ADDITIVES

The two most common additives to coffee are chicory and fig, although in the Middle East spices such as cardamom, ginger, cinnamon and nutmeg are frequently added, either during the last few minutes of roasting or during brewing.

Chicory is favoured by the French, and 'French blends and roasts' frequently have it added. Fig seasoning is mainly added in Austria and most coffee described as 'Viennese' has the addition of fig.

COFFEE GRINDING

Ideally one should grind coffee beans just before brewing, as ground coffee starts to lose its flavour almost immediately, and there is a noticeable loss after an hour.

There are a variety of different grinders on the market, of which the simplest and possibly the best are the manual ones. They vary considerably in design, but the basic principle behind them all is the same; rather like an old-fashioned mincer, which some of them resemble. The beans are fed through, a few at a time, as the handle is turned and the blades grind the beans into a drawer below. Depending on the sophistication of the machine, the blades can be adjusted to give different grinds.

Electric grinders which work on this principle are also available, but are generally rather expensive. The more common kind are the ones with two blades which whizz round and, in effect, 'chop' the beans. The biggest disadvantage of this method is that it is easy to get an uneven grind, with some of the beans becoming almost pulverised whilst others remain quite coarse. It is best only to grind a small amount at a time. With most food processors and blenders this problem is exaggerated.

The grind of coffee required depends on the way in which it is to be brewed in order to extract the maximum flavour.

Pulverised, which is ground almost as fine as flour, is used only for Turkish coffee.

Very Fine is used for paper filters and espresso.

Fine is used for other methods of filter, such as the French drip pot and for the vacuum method.

Medium is used for the Italian Neapolitan and for the plunger or cafetière.

Coarse is used for the jug method.

STORING COFFEE

Other than green beans, coffee shold not be stored for any length of time. The basic rule, no matter what kind of coffee – beans, ground, even instant – is that it should be stored in an airtight tin or jar. This (a) prevents oxygen from circulating freely round the coffee into which it loses its flavour and aroma, and (b) prevents the coffee from being contaminated by other flavours and smells which it quickly absorbs. Roast beans can be kept in this way for a month, but grounds should be used within a week.

Roast coffee beans will, in fact, keep marginally better if placed in a heavy-gauge polythene bag in a freezer for up to a month. Although some of the branded ground coffees do advise storing in the refrigerator once the vacuum has been broken, most experts agree that there is not a great deal to gained from this.

How To Make A Good Cup Of coffee

1. *The coffee:* This should be as fresh as possible. The more recently roasted and ground the beans, the better the end result will be. Use the correct ratio of coffee to water (see below).

2. *The water:* This should be freshly drawn. Soft water makes a better cup of coffee than hard water, but do not use water that has been artificially softened. Do not make coffee with boiling water, ideally it should be at 94°C/200°F.

3. *Cleanliness:* All the utensils should be scrupulously clean. It is only too easy to leave a few grounds behind or not wash the container too carefully and coffee stains and remains of old coffee can taint a fresh brew.

4. Serve the coffee as soon as possible after it has been brewed. Coffee that has been left to 'stew' quickly acquires a bitter flavour.

5. Never allow the coffee to boil.

6. Never re-heat coffee. The only way in which coffee has been found to re-heat with any real degree of success is in a microwave.

7. *Ratio of coffee to water:* The exact amount of coffee required depends both on individual taste and on the method of brewing. It is *not* related to the type of coffee used. If you reduce the amount of a strong, Continental roast, you will not get a round-bodied but weaker cup of coffee, you will get a thin-tasting, rather bitter one.

If a fine grind of coffee is used, as in the filter method, slightly less coffee is needed than if you are using a coarser grind, suitable for the jug and plunger methods. This is because it is easier to extract the flavour from coffee that is more finely ground. Generally the best results are obtained if you use one rounded tablespoon of ground coffee for every 225 ml/8 fl oz cup of water.

METHODS OF BREWING

The way you brew your coffee is entirely a matter of choice. The one common method which is *not* recommended is the percolator, because this involves boiling the coffee which ruins it, making it bitter and acrid.

Jug: The most basic, but some consider the most superior method. The jug should be warmed, then either stood on a hot plate or in a saucepan of boiling water off the heat. Put the grounds in the jug and add enough almost boiling water (water which has boiled and then been left to stand for two minutes to lower the temperature slightly) to wet them thoroughly. Leave for a minute before pouring over the remainder of the water. Stir well, cover and leave to stand for about eight minutes. Skim the surface with a spoon to remove excess grounds, then leave for a further minute to allow all the grounds to sink to the bottom before straining into cups.

Cafetière or plunger: This works on the same principle as the jug method and consists of a glass, heatproof jug and a fine-meshed plunger which pushes the grounds to the bottom of the pot. Infuse for four to six minutes, before pushing the plunger down to the bottom of the jug. Always use a medium grind.

Filter: Possibly the simplest method, certainly for a novice. Filters come in various sizes from single cup to larger ones which fit over a jug or pot and are lined with a conical paper bag. The cup or jug should first be warmed, and a large jug needs to be kept warm. Place the coffee in the bottom of the paper liner and pour on enough water to wet the grounds. Leave for a minute, then gradually add more water as it drips through the grounds.

Electric Filter: This is an automated version of the above method and one that has rapidly gained popularity in the last few years. Cold water is poured into a reservoir, an electric element heats a small amount of it at a time to the correct temperature and pours it on to the coffee grounds, where it drips through to a jug on a hotplate.

French Filter Pot: When this is ready for serving it looks almost exactly like a teapot. When brewing, a tube, the same size as the lid of the pot, sits on top of it and the water is poured into it. The coffee is in a section between the two parts. It works in exactly the same way as the filter method.

Neapolitan: Next to expresso, this is the most common form of brewing in Italy. The biggest problem with it, is that many models are made of aluminium, which has a tendency to taint the coffee. It works on a filter basis and consists of two pots placed one on top of the other. Cold water is placed in the bottom pot, into which slots a container with grounds; the other pot, which has a spout, is placed on the top. The water is brought to the boil, removed from the heat and allowed to stand for two minutes, then the pots are turned upside down, which allows the water to drip through into the other pot, which becomes the serving pot.

Vacuum method: A method that was extremely popular, but has lost ground to both the cafetière and automatic electric filters, largely due to expense. It consists of two glass bowls, which fit on top of each other, and a filter which goes between the two bowls. The cold water is placed in the lower bowl, which is used for serving, the coffee is added to the upper bowl. The machine is placed over heat. When the water in the lower bowl starts to boil it rises up into the upper bowl, and when it is removed from the heat the coffee filters back down into the lower bowl.

Microwave coffee makers: These work on exactly the same principle as the vacuum method, but all the components are made of heat-resistant plastic so there is no risk of overheating.

Espresso: For many coffee buffs, this is the ultimate method of brewing. Instead of water dripping through the coffee, steam and water are forced quickly through the coffee grounds under pressure, which extracts the maximum flavour from the beans. Although domestic versions of the kind of machines one sees in coffee bars and restaurants are available, they are expensive and if you like coffee brewed in this way it is possible to buy a small pot which works on the same principle.

Espresso coffee is always served black in small cups which can be decorated with a twist of lemon, or it can be topped with frothy milk to make it into cappucino, which usually has a little cocoa or drinking chocolate sprinkled over the top.

Turkish coffee: This is definitely an acquired taste as it is very thick, strong and almost syrupy. It should really be made in an ibrik, a tall narrow container, usually made of copper with a long handle, but you can use any small, high-sided saucepan. For each cup required, use a small cup of water, a heaped teaspoon of pulverised coffee and a heaped teaspoon of sugar. Place the sugar and water in the pan and bring to the boil. Remove from the heat, stir in the coffee and bring it back to the boil. As soon as the coffee has boiled, remove it from the heat and tap the base gently until the froth subsides. Repeat this twice more. After the last boiling, remove from the heat and spoon some of the creamy froth into each cup before pouring the coffee slowly out of the pan. If liked, a cardamom seed can be added to each cup, or the coffee can be served with a stick of cinnamon.

———————◆———————

COFFEE LIQUEURS

There are two main liqueurs made from coffee – Kahluá and Tia Maria. The former is of Mexican origin, whilst the latter is of Jamaican, but the methods of making them remain closely guarded secrets. Both can be used to make a number of different cocktails, and two of the best are Black Russian and Brandy Alexander.

BLACK RUSSIAN: Mix 2 parts vodka with 1 part coffee liqueur and pour over some ice cubes in a glass. Serve on its own, or top up with Coca Cola.

BRANDY ALEXANDER: Put 1 part cream, 1 part coffee liqueur and 1 part brandy in a cocktail shaker with some crushed ice. Mix in the shaker and strain into a glass.

HOT COFFEE DRINKS

GAELIC (OR IRISH) COFFEE: Put a heaped teaspoon of sugar in the bottom of a warmed wine glass. Stir in a measure of whisk(e)y, then fill to within about 1 inch of the top with strong, hot, black coffee. Stir well so that the sugar is mixed with the coffee as this plays a key part in ensuring that the cream remains on the top. Holding a dessertspoon over the coffee, carefully pour some double cream over the back of the spoon. Serve at once.

COFFEE BALALAIKA is a variation of Gaelic Coffee using vodka in place of the whisk(e)y.

CAFÉ BRÛLOT is another popular fortified drink. For each cup of coffee you need 2 teaspoons sugar, 3 cloves, a strip each of lemon and orange peel, a 1 inch stick of cinnamon and a good measure of brandy. Pour the hot coffee into a warmed cup. Gently heat all the other ingredients together in a small saucepan, and when the sugar has dissolved, set it alight and pour it into the coffee.

CAFÉ ROYALE is simply strong, sweetened black coffee with a generous measure of brandy added to it.

HAPPY MARRIAGE is popular in various parts of the Continent, particularly in Switzerland and Germany. It is a mixture of equal parts coffee and hot chocolate, either on its own or with a little brandy or rum added.

ICED COFFEE DRINKS

O n a hot day, iced coffee is one of the most refreshing drinks one can have. The most usual iced coffee is equal quantities of milk and double strength coffee, although strong sweetened black coffee poured over some ice cubes is equally delicious.

SPICED ICED COFFEE: Brew about 1 pint double strength black coffee, and pour over 2 cinnamon sticks, 6 cloves, 6 allspice berries and a tablespoon of sugar. Leave to stand for at least 1 hour. Taste and add more sugar if necessary. Pour over some ice cubes in four glasses and top each one with a swirl of whipped cream.

CAFÉ LIÈGOISE: Brew double strength coffee and sweeten to taste. Pour over ice cubes in tall glasses and fill three-quarters full. Add a scoopful of vanilla or coffee ice cream and top each glass with a swirl of whipped cream sprinkled with a little chocolate powder.

COFFEE MILK SHAKE: This rather simpler drink will be popular with children. Dissolve 2 teaspoons instant coffee and 1 teaspoon sugar in 1 tablespoon hot water. Put into a blender with 1/4 pint cold milk and 3 scoopfuls vanilla ice cream. Mix until smooth and frothy, then pour into a tall glass and serve with a straw.

INSTANT COFFEE

I nstant coffee accounts for over 80% of the coffee drunk in the United Kingdom. It was first marketed by an Englishman, Mr G. Washington, in 1909. Three years earlier, while sitting in his garden in Guatemala waiting for his wife to join him for coffee after lunch, he noticed a fine powder on the spout of the silver coffee pot. This he realised must have been caused by the evaporation of the steam, so he set about finding ways in which it could be done commercially.

To a coffee connoisseur, instant coffee is not coffee at all, and Mr Washington did coffee a great disservice by his discovery. But increasingly sophisticated methods of manufacture does mean that at the top end of the instant coffee market you may well have a drink which is superior to badly brewed fresh coffee, even if this has been made with quality beans. Instant coffee has the distinct advantage that it can make the cheaper grades of coffee actually taste better than they would if they were roast and ground.

There are two methods of manufacturing instant coffee, but in both of them the coffee beans are roasted and ground in the usual way, and great vats of coffee brewed. In the newer, better (and more expensive), method of freeze drying, the liquid coffee is frozen in slabs which are ground up into small particles. The ice is then vaporised straight into steam, leaving behind granules of dry coffee.

In the original and more common method, the liquid coffee is 'spray dried' in heated towers, which results either in a fine powder or small granules. As considerable heat is required, it has the same effect as boiling coffee and some of the flavour and all the 'aroma' are driven off. To replace this, the powder or granules are then sprayed with a concentrated 'coffee essence or oil'.

COFFEE ESSENCE

Manufacturers of coffee essence are somewhat reluctant to divulge how it is made, which is apt to make one rather suspicious as to its content. However, although it is not pleasant to drink, it can be useful for some coffee recipes when you wish to add a strong coffee flavour without adding excessive liquid. It also gives a consistent result.

CAFFEINE

From the moment when roasted coffee beans were first made into a drink, the debate has raged as to whether or not coffee is good or evil. In England, in the late seventeenth century, one physician claimed it cured just about every disease from scurvy and dropsy to migraine, whilst another vigorously declared that drunk with milk it caused leprosy! With such far-fetched claims being made on either side, in Germany as well as in England, Bach was inspired to compose his Coffee Cantata, which mocks these incessant discussions.

One of the reasons why the Swedes are the second biggest coffee drinkers in the world (only exceeded by their neighbours Finland) is because, in the eighteenth century, King Gustav III thought he would settle the controversy between coffee and tea once and for all. A pair of identical twins were condemned to death for murder, but he commuted their sentences to life imprisonment on the understanding that every day one was to be given several large cups of coffee to drink and other other several large cups of tea. The tea drinker died first – at the age of 83!

A link has frequently been made between coffee and longevity. A Russian scientist, Il'ya Machnikov, was convinced that coffee had played an important part in the lives of a number of Russian centenarians. Elizabeth Durieux of Savoy, who lived to the great age of 114, reputedly drank 40 small cups a day. And there is an old Bourbon proverb which perhaps sums up what a great many people feel about coffee:

'To an old man, a cup of coffee is like the down post of an old house, it sustains and strengthens it.'

The effect of caffeine is to stimulate the central nervous system, so that the heart rate is slightly increased and the blood vessels dilate. The average cup of coffee contains about 100 milligrams of caffeine – the same as a can of cola – whilst tea contains 70. In moderation, this stimulation is generally considered beneficial, but if taken to excess it can have a toxic effect.

Because caffeine stimulates and sharpens the senses, rather than deadening them as alcohol does, coffee has always been beloved by the thinkers and writers. Balzac, for example, who drank between 20 and 30 cups a day, said, 'It makes ideas begin to move like the battalions of the Grande Armée', Voltaire said that if coffee was a poison 'I have been poisoning myself for more than 50 years and am not yet dead', whilst Alexander Pope, who composed a number of poems about coffee, wrote:

'Coffee surely makes the politician wise, And see through all things with his half-shut eyes.'

Napoleon, aware that it was a great deal better for his troops than alcohol, made coffee the official military drink, and said of it, 'Strong coffee, and plenty, awakens me. It gives me a warmth, an unusual force, a pain, that is not without pleasure. I would rather suffer than be senseless.' And it was said by an American General after the First World War that coffee, together with bread and bacon, had been the 3 nutritional essentials that had won the war for the Allies.

Many of the accusations that have been levelled against coffee in the past were stirred up by other interested parties. Coffee has been claimed to be an aphrodisiac, but in Marseilles in the middle of the seventeenth century the wine trade was very quick to circulate a story from Persia claiming that coffee caused impotence. It was said that one of the Persian kings drank so much coffee that he completely lost his interest in women. One day the queen saw a stallion being gelded, and on asking why this had been necessary was informed that he had become too excitable and difficult to handle with so many mares about. To which she replied that it would have been much easier just to give him plenty of coffee to drink every day. Hardly surprisingly, amongst the virile Southern French, this story had a disastrous effect on the coffee trade!

In exactly the same way as some people have a much stronger head for alcohol than others, the amount of coffee which you can drink without it affecting you adversely is entirely up to the individual. As well as being dependent on the type of coffee being drunk, the time of day and also the state of mind you are in when you drink it will have an effect.

DE-CAFFEINATED COFFEE

For people who enjoy the taste of coffee but find they are susceptible to the effects of caffeine, there are now several varieties of de-caffeinated coffees on the market, both roasted beans and instant coffees.

Caffeine is actually tasteless, so removing it from the bean prior to roasting should not, in principle, affect the flavour of the coffee at all. As it is water soluble, it is also not difficult to remove it from the bean. The problem centres round removing it while at the same time keeping the precious flavourings of the coffee intact. Various methods are used to do this.

The solvent method, in which the beans are soaked in hot water for several hours, is the most usual. The water is then strained off into tanks, where it is combined with a solvent which absorbs caffeine. The solvent is separated from the water, which therefore becomes free of both caffeine and solvent, but still contains some of the essential coffee flavourings. The beans are then put back into the water so that the flavourings can be re-absorbed.

The caffeine is sold for use in medicines and to soft drink manufacturers, so in theory everything should be perfect. But many people who are health conscious worry about the chemicals used in the solvent. Experiments are being carried out to try to find chemical-free ways of removing the caffeine.

FOLKLORE AND RITUAL

* Throughout the Arab world, coffee is a symbol of hospitality, and in Southern Egypt and Uganda beans are exchanged as a friendly greeting.

* The Arabs are so fussy about the way their coffee is made that, although food is supplied to Saudi Airlines in New York, London and other major cities, the Arabic coffee is made only in Jeddah and is flown round the world in Thermos flasks.

* The Arabs have a coffee ceremony, which is not dissimilar to the better known Japanese tea ceremony. The guests sit on mats on the floor, the coffee is roasted with cardamom in a fireplace at one end of the room, and the nearer you are placed to the fire, the more honoured a guest you are. After roasting, the coffee is ground in a pestle and mortar before being made into a thick, spicy brew. A little is then poured into a cup to warm it, and from there to the next cup. When it has been used to warm all the cups, this coffee is thrown on the floor as an offering to Shadhilly, the patron saint of coffee drinkers. The cups are then filled half full – to fill them to the brim is considered an insult to the guest bidding him or her to leave. As the server hands the cups round he says *semm* (say the name of God), to which the guest replies *bismillah* (to God) before drinking the coffee.

* Coffee has replaced alcohol in the Moslem world, where it is known as the 'wine of Apollo'. It was first used by the dervishes to keep them awake during prayer, and in these countries there is still a strong association between coffee and rituals and religion.

* A visitor to Cairo in the early sixteenth century described how one of the dervishes from the Yemen kept a large, red earthenware vessel of coffee brewing during prayers. This was handed out to the congregation during the service as they chanted 'There is no God, but one God, the true king, whose power is not to be disputed.'

* Coffee has for so long been considered such an essential part of Turkish life that the sight of coffee beggars used to be quite normal, and not to offer someone one met in the street a cup of coffee was the height of bad manners.

* When a Turkish man asked a father for his daughter's hand in marriage he had to promise him that this bride would never go short of coffee. Indeed, if she did, it was legitimate grounds for divorce.

* As Turkish and Arabic coffee is not strained, the grounds left in the cup are used to tell fortunes in the same way in which tea leaves are used in other parts of the world. There is also a method of fortune telling whereby the fortune teller makes the client hold the coffee cup as tight as he can while the fortune is being told, and then the coffee is thrown on the floor as an offering to Shadhilly.

* Although it has sometimes been accused of causing infertility, in Africa the beans are frequently used in witchcraft and in fertility rites. One tribe has a blood brother ceremony in which the blood of the two people is mixed and put between the two seeds of the coffee fruit, which are then eaten.

COOKING WITH COFFEE

C offee has been used in baking and for desserts almost as long as people have been drinking it, but what is perhaps more surprising is that it can be used in savoury dishes. A savoury coffee dish does not, and should not, taste distinctively of coffee, but a small quantity can do much to enhance the flavour of the other ingredients.

In the following recipes where strong black and very strong black coffee are referred to, strong black means an after-dinner strength, whilst very strong means espresso strength or double strength.

Apart from the obvious coffee recipes, a number of homely, everyday standbys like bread and butter pudding can be varied by replacing some of the fluid with coffee. This is a good way of using up any left-over brewed coffee.

BRAZILIAN BEEF

Like a number of casseroles, this one improves with keeping, and is at its best when made the day before and reheated.

3 tablespoons oil
2 lb braising beef, cubed
2 large onions, peeled and sliced
2 cloves garlic, crushed
2 green peppers, seeded and sliced
1 oz flour
¼ pint dry white wine
scant ½ pint black coffee
1 teaspoon dried oregano
salt and freshly milled black pepper

Heat the oil in a pan and quickly fry the meat until browned. Remove from the pan with a draining spoon and put on one side. Add the onions, garlic and peppers to the fat remaining in the pan and fry gently for 10 minutes.

Sprinkle over the flour and cook for 2–3 minutes, stirring frequently. Gradually stir in the wine and coffee and bring to the boil, stirring all the time. Add the oregano and seasoning and replace the meat.

Cover and simmer gently for 1½–2 hours or until the meat is very tender. Taste and adjust the seasoning before serving.

Serves 6

CHICKEN STROGANOFF

A more economical version of the classic Russian Beef Stroganoff. The coffee just gives it a little added extra flavour.

1¼ lb chicken breasts
salt and freshly milled black pepper
1 oz butter
1 large onion, peeled and finely chopped
4 oz mushrooms, sliced
1 tablespoon tomato purée
4 tablespoons very strong black coffee
¼ teaspoon dried thyme
¼ pint soured cream

Cut the chicken into thin strips, about ¼ inch thick and 2 inches long. Season with salt and pepper. Melt the butter in a large frying pan and gently fry the onion for 5 minutes. Add the mushrooms and cook for a further 2 minutes.

Increase the heat, add the chicken and cook, stirring, for a further 2–3 minutes. Blend the tomato purée with the coffee and add to the pan with the thyme. Mix well and continue cooking for further 2 minutes. Stir in the cream and heat gently without allowing the mixture to boil. Taste and adjust the seasoning and serve with boiled rice or noodles.

Serves 4

STUFFED MUSHROOMS

Although almost impossible to detect in the finished dish, the coffee definitely adds something to this delicious starter.

6 large flat mushrooms
2 oz butter
1 medium-sized onion, peeled and chopped
2 cloves garlic, crushed
5 oz fresh wholemeal breadcrumbs
8 oz pork sausagement
2 tablespoons chopped parsley
1 teaspoon dried thyme or rosemary
3 tablespoons strong black coffee
salt and freshly milled black pepper

Remove the stalks from the mushrooms and arrange in a single layer, gills side up, in a buttered dish. Chop the stalks.

Melt 1 oz butter in a small pan and gently fry the onion, garlic and chopped mushrooms stalks until the onions are soft. Remove from the heat, turn into a bowl and add all the remaining ingredients, except the butter. Mix well. Divide the stuffing into six and pile on top of the mushrooms. Dot with the remaining butter. If you wish to prepare the mushrooms in advance they can be left at this stage.

Bake in a moderate oven, 180°C/350°F/Gas 4 for 40 minutes. Serve hot.

Serves 6

COFFEE ZABAGLIONE

An interesting American variation of a well-known (and well-loved) recipe.

2 egg yolks
2 oz caster sugar
2 tablespoons dark rum
4 fl oz very strong black coffee

Place the egg yolks and sugar in a bowl and whisk until thick and creamy. Add the rum, place over a pan of gently simmering water and continue whisking until thick. Then gradually whisk in the coffee until you have a thick creamy mixture in which the whisk will leave a good trail when lifted out of it.

Pour into two glasses and serve at once with crisp biscuits.

Serves 2

MOCHA MOUSSE

By adding coffee to chocolate dishes, it makes them a little more 'bitter' and therefore you can use less expensive chocolate and cake coverings.

4 oz plain chocolate cake covering
1 rounded tablespoon instant coffee granules
1 tablespoon water or 1–2 tablespoons dark rum
4 eggs, separated

Break the chocolate into pieces and put into a basin with the coffee and water or rum. Stand the basin over a pan of hot water and leave until the chocolate has melted.

Remove from heat and beat in the egg yolks, one at a time. Whisk the egg whites until they form stiff peaks, then fold into the chocolate mixture. Turn into a serving dish and chill for at least 1 hour before serving.

Serves 4

PETITS POTS DE CRÈME AU CAFÉ

These deliciously rich little custards need to be served well chilled. They are excellent topped with fresh fruit, such as a strawberry or two or three raspberries.

¼ pint double strength black coffee
½ pint double cream
3 egg yolks
1 oz vanilla sugar

Heat the coffee and cream to just below boiling point. Beat the egg yolks with the sugar until thick and creamy, then pour over the hot coffee and cream. Mix well, and strain into 4 individual china dishes or ramekins.

Stand dishes in a roasting tin containing 1 inch cold water and bake in a low oven, 150°C/300°F/Gas 2 for about 40 minutes, or until the custards are just set. Remove from the oven, allow to cool, then chill.

Serves 4

STEAMED COFFEE PUDDING

A really light steamed pudding which can either be served with whipped cream flavoured with coffee liqueur, or with a hot Sabayon or Coffee Butterscotch Sauce (see opposite).

¼ pint double cream
4 tablespoons very strong black coffee
5 oz white breadcrumbs
4 oz butter
2 oz ground almonds
4 oz caster sugar
4 eggs, beaten

Blend the cream with the coffee, pour over the breadcrumbs and leave to soak for 10 minutes, then beat well.

Cream the butter, then, preferably using an electric mixer, beat in the breadcrumb mixture, almonds and sugar and continue beating until the mixture is smooth. Gradually beat in the eggs, a little at a time.

Turn into a buttered 2 pint pudding basin. Cover with a double layer of buttered greaseproof paper or foil and steam for 2 hours, remembering to check from time to time that the pan is not boiling dry. Turn out of the bowl and serve hot.

Serves 4–6

SABAYON SAUCE

2 egg yolks
2 oz caster sugar
a good pinch of arrowroot
4 fl oz strong black coffee

Whisk the egg yolks, sugar and arrowroot in a basin until thick and white. Place the basin over a pan of gently simmering water and gradually whisk in the coffee until the mixture is thick and leaves a trail when lifted out of the mixture.

Serves 4–6

COFFEE AND BUTTERSCOTCH SAUCE

1 tablespoon cornflour
3 tablespoons soft brown sugar
½ pint milk
1 tablespoon instant coffee granules
1 oz unsalted butter

Blend the cornflour and sugar in a basin and stir in 3 tablespoons of the milk to make a smooth paste. Bring the remaining milk and the coffee to the boil and pour over the blended cornflour, stirring all the time. Return to the pan and bring back to the boil, stirring all the time. Remove from the heat, add the butter and stir until it has melted.

Serve hot with steamed puddings or ice cream.

Serves 4–6

CHARLOTTE MALAKOFF

A true 'Queen of Puddings'. This makes the perfect ending for any dinner party.

6 oz butter
5 oz caster sugar
5 tablespoons coffee liqueur
1/4 pint very strong black coffee
4 oz ground almonds
1/4 pint double cream
1/4 pint single cream
3 tablespoons water
about 32 Boudoir or sponge finger biscuits

To decorate:
1/4 pint double cream
roast coffee beans

Line the base of a 7-inch loose-bottomed cake tin with buttered greaseproof or silicone paper.

Cream together the butter and sugar until light and fluffy. Blend together 3 tablespoons of the liqueur with 3 tablespoons of the coffee. Gradually beat this into the creamed mixture alternately with the almonds. Whip the double and single cream together until it holds its shape, then fold into the mixture.

Add the remaining liqueur and the water to the remaining coffee. Trim the sponge fingers so that they are the same height as the tin. Dip each sponge finger quickly in the coffee and use to line the sides of the cake tin; place the rounded end down and the sugar-coated side out. When you have finished lining the tin, soak any remaining biscuits, together with the trimmed ends, in the coffee.

Spread half the almond mixture over the base of the prepared tin, and cover with the soaked sponge fingers. Spread the last of the almond mixture on top. Lay a piece of buttered greaseproof or silicone paper over the charlotte, cover with a small plate and place a weight on top to press it down. Chill for at least 4 hours or overnight until the mixture is quite firm.

Invert the charlotte on to a serving plate and remove the tin. Whip the double cream until it is stiff and pipe over the top of the charlotte. Decorate with coffee beans.

Serves 8–10

GRANITA

A dark, Continental roast is used to make this water ice, which, as its name implies, should be slightly granular in texture. You can serve it on its own, or it can be topped with a spoonful of whipped cream or vanilla ice cream and a tablespoon of coffee liqueur.

3 oz ground coffee
1 pint boiling water
¼ pint cold water
5 oz granulated sugar

Place the coffee grounds in a jug, and stand the jug in a saucepan of water over a very low heat. Pour the boiling water into the jug, stir well, then leave the coffee to infuse for 30 minutes. Strain through a piece of muslin or a filter paper into a bowl.

Put the cold water and granulated sugar in a small pan, place over a gentle heat until the sugar has melted, then increase the heat, bring to the boil and boil for 5 minutes. Remove from the heat, add to the coffee and mix well. Allow to cool.

Place the bowl in the freezer and freeze, removing the bowl every 30 minutes to whisk the mixture to prevent ice crystals from forming. Once the granita is frozen, transfer to a plastic or other suitable container, cover and keep until required.

Serves 4

COFFEE AND WALNUT CAKE

Coffee has a natural affinity with all nuts.

For the cake:
6 oz butter
6 oz light soft brown sugar
3 eggs, beaten
6 oz self-raising flour
2 tablespoons coffee essence
3 oz walnuts, finely chopped

For the filling and topping:
4 oz butter
6 oz icing sugar, sifted
3 tablespoons very strong black coffee
about 10 walnut halves

Grease and line 2 × 7 inch sandwich tins. Cream the butter and sugar together until very light and fluffy, then gradually beat in the eggs, adding a tablespoon of flour with the last amount of egg. Sift in the rest of the flour and fold in, then fold in the coffee essence and walnuts. Divide the mixture between the two tins and bake at 180°C/350°F/Gas 4 for 20–25 minutes or until the cakes spring back when lightly pressed. Remove from the oven, leave in the tins for 2–3 minutes, then turn out and cool on a wire rack.

Cream the butter and gradually beat in the sugar alternately with the coffee. Spread half the mixture over one of the cakes, sandwich them together, then spread the remaining butter icing over the top, swirling it up with a fork. Decorate with walnut halves.

Rum Soaked Gâteau

An old favourite but one that nevertheless is always popular.

8-inch Victoria Sandwich or Madeira Cake

For the rum syrup:
6 oz soft brown sugar
¾ pint strong black coffee
3 tablespoons dark rum

To decorate:
¼ pint single cream
¼ pint double cream
roast coffee beans

To make the syrup, put the sugar and coffee into a pan over a low heat and leave until the sugar has dissolved. Remove from the heat and stir in the rum. Put the cake on a serving plate and pierce it all over with a skewer and pour over some of the hot syrup. As the cake absorbs the syrup, pour over a little more until it has all been used. Leave to stand for at least 2 hours, or up to 12.

Whip the double and single cream together until it holds its shape, then spread all over the cake, swirling it up into peaks. Decorate with coffee beans.

COFFEE AND DATE LOAF

A simple 'tea bread' delicious sliced and spread with butter.

8 oz self-raising flour
1 teaspoon baking powder
2 oz soft margarine
2 tablespoons honey
6 oz dates, chopped
7 tablespoons milk
1 tablespoon instant coffee granules

Well grease a 1 lb loaf tin. Sift the flour and baking powder into a bowl. Add all the remaining ingredients and beat well for 1 minute. Turn into the prepared tin and level off. Bake in a moderately hot oven, 190°C/375°F/Gas 5, for about 50 minutes or until well risen and a skewer inserted into the centre of the loaf comes out clean. Leave in the tin for 2–3 minutes, then turn out and cool on a wire rack.

COFFEE FUDGE

Despite, or perhaps because of, being wickedly fattening, homemade fudge is a surefire winner. You can vary this one by adding chopped nuts and/or some raisins.

1/4 pint milk
2 tablespoons instant coffee granules
1 lb granulated sugar
3 oz butter

Well butter a shallow a 7 inch square cake tin. Pour the milk into a large, heavy-based pan, add the coffee granules, and stir until almost all the coffee has dissolved. Add the sugar and the butter.

Place the pan over a gentle heat, stirring until the sugar has dissolved, then increase the heat and boil rapidly to 118°C/240°F, or until a small amount of the mixture forms a soft ball when dropped into a basin of cold water. Stir once or twice to prevent the mixture from burning.

Remove from the heat and allow to cool for about 3 minutes, then beat hard until the mixture becomes thick and creamy. Pour immediately into the prepared tin. When it is beginning to set, mark the fudge into squares with a sharp knife, then cut when completely cold.

Makes just over 1 lb

OTHER USES FOR COFFEE

* Coffee grounds are not generally put to a great many other uses, although as they are rich in minerals and vitamins they can be used for fertilising plants, so long as the plants like acidic soil.

* In parts of Africa, the berries are allowed to ferment to make a coffee wine, whilst in Ethiopia they used to toast the leaves and make them into a kind of flour.

BEAUTY TREATMENTS

* In Japan, people bathe in a mixture of ground coffee and fermented pineapple pulp to cleanse and enrich the skin. People are immersed, up to their necks, in the mixture and remain in it for about an hour. As the pineapple pulp ferments it gives off heat, so that a similar effect to a sauna is created.

* The grounds can also be steeped in hot water for several hours, then strained and mixed with henna to give a rich, reddy brown hair colouring. As coffee, like henna, is a natural product, this is an exceptionally good way of dyeing hair which is starting to grey.

MEDICINAL USE

* In Mrs Cadogan's Cookbook of recipes for *The Irish RM* there is an old Irish remedy for curing a headache (or a hangover?): Squeeze the juice of half a lemon into a cup of sugarless black coffee and drink it.

* Writing in the 'North American Review' in 1889, a Charles K. Tuckerman swore that an elderly relative who was dying before his very eyes, having eaten and drunk nothing for days, was virtually brought back from the dead by a glass of hot black coffee mixed with an egg yolk. But one must concede that this was probably an exceptional case!

* Researchers at Bristol University have found that the caffeine in a strong cup of instant coffee will inhibit the herpes virus and make cold sores disappear more quickly. Make a strong cup of coffee and dab it on the affected place with cotton wool. It is thought that shingles may also react to an ointment of caffeine.

HOUSEHOLD USES

* In Lapland they use coffee beans as counters in a game called Taplo, which is similar to backgammon. If you use green beans, they make very good cheap counters for a number of games. They can also be used for making collages, or as fillings for rattles, but do try not to let young children or babies get hold of the beans as they would be easy to choke on.

* Three or four freshly roasted coffee beans placed in the ashtray of a car will help to absorb the smell of the cigarette smoke and ash, and help the car to smell fresher.

* Used grounds can be used for dyeing, and this is a good way to give an extra lease of life to an old T-shirt. You need between 1–2 lb grounds, depending on the weight of clothes you plan to dye and how dark you want the end result to be.

  The grounds should be firmly tied in a double piece of muslin and placed in a large tub with 3–4 gallons of water, 3 tablespoons salt and 1 tablespoon washing soda. Bring to the boil and boil gently for about 10 minutes to extract some of the dye from the grounds, then add the clothes and boil gently for about 20 minutes or until the desired colour is reached. Rinse until the water is clear, then dry.

  If you prefer you can use a washing machine on the hottest wash, and this often gives a more even dyeing.

As A Houseplant

* A few enterprising coffee addicts with large green-houses have managed to grow enough coffee trees to provide a decent crop. That, however, is not practical for 99.9% of the population, but the Arabica does make an attractive houseplant which will, if carefully nurtured, produce some fruit.

You can sometimes buy the plants from a nursery, or you can grow them from seed, if you plant green beans in some potting compost and water them well. They take up to four weeks to germinate and the success rate is likely to be limited. The plants like a rich, well-drained soil in a warm, light, airy atmosphere with indirect sunlight. Good luck.

Acknowledgements

Grateful acknowledgement is made to the London Coffee Information centre for their invaluable help and assistance.